french
cuisine

Chef
express

Published by:
TRIDENT PRESS INTERNATIONAL
801 12th Avenue South, Suite 400
Naples, Fl 34102 USA
Tel: + 1 239 649 7077
Fax: + 1 239 649 5832
Email: tridentpress@worldnet.att.net
Websites: www.trident-international.com
www.chefexpressinternational.com

French cuisine
© Trident Press

Publishers: Simon St. John Bailey and
Elaine S. Evans
Editor-in-chief: Isabel Toyos

Texts
Editing and supervision: Aurora Giribaldi
Translation: Sandra Heyman
Proofreading: Rosa Corgatelli

Design and layout
Cover: Matilde Bossi
Inside: M&A Gráfica
Step by step photography: Fernando Giampieri
Step by step styling: Emi Pechar

Prepress
Mikonos Comunicación Gráfica

All rights reserved. No part of this book may be stored, reproduced or transmitted in any form and by any means without written permission of the Publisher, except in the case of brief quotations embodied in critical articles and reviews.

Includes Index
ISBN 1582796661
UPC 6 15269 96661 7

First Edition Printed in February 2004

Printed in Peru by Quebecor

introduction

In this book you will find recipes that retain the wonderful flavors of classic French cooking, but do not require the time, or contain the calories, of this popular cuisine. The emphasis is on fresh food that tastes wonderful, looks great and is easy to prepare. The food is not 'nouvelle cuisine' but, rather, traditional French-style food

french cuisine
introduction

adapted to suit today's lifestyles. The recipes are light, fresh and interesting, and use the healthier cooking techniques such as grilling, baking and poaching.

From the sea

The coastline of France and especially that of the Mediterranean are rich in fish and seafood, and it is from these areas that many of today's popular seafood dishes come. You will find colorful bouillabaisse –the most famous fish soup around the world, which can be considered either as a great starter or as a complete one-dish meal– and aromatic mussels in wine and garlic –perfect to tempt the tastebuds.

Poultry plates

Traditional recipes such as coq au vin and duck a l'orange are made using considerably less fat, yet retain their authentic flavors.

Meat at its best

The selection of meat recipes shows the diversity of French cooking. Pot-au-feu is wonderful for feeding a crowd, while sausages with onions and wine is a perfect family meal and steak bordelaise an easy dish for mid-week entertaining.

Vegetable dishes

These are an important part of French cooking. In southern France they are often the main dish, while in other areas they enhance or complement a meat, fish, poultry or game dish. The recipes in this book are ideal for vegetarian meals, and many make imaginative first courses.

Perfect finishes

Many of the best French desserts are fruit based. Here you will find a selection of light desserts that won't ruin your diet... and a wonderful chocolate soufflé to indulge your guests.

Difficulty scale

■□□ I Easy to do

■■□ I Requires attention

■■■ I Requires experience

french
onion soup

Cooking time: 35 minutes - Preparation time: 8 minutes

ingredients
- 60 g/2 oz butter
- 4 onions, thinly sliced
- 2 teaspoons flour
- 4 cups/1 liter/1¾ pt chicken stock
- ½ cup/125 ml/4 fl oz white wine
- 8 slices French bread, toasted
- 60 g/2 oz grated Gruyère cheese

method
1. Melt butter in a large saucepan, add onions and cook over a low heat, stirring constantly, for 10-15 minutes or until onions are golden. Stir in flour and cook, stirring, for 5 minutes longer.
2. Increase heat to medium, stir in stock and wine and bring to the boil, then reduce heat and simmer for 10 minutes.
3. Top toasted bread with cheese and cook under a preheated grill for 2-3 minutes or until cheese melts. Place cheese toast in the base of a large soup tureen and pour over soup. Serve immediately.

Serves 4

tip from the chef

An alternative serving suggestion is to place two slices of toast in each soup bowl, then pour over the soup.

soups and starters > 7

8 > FRENCH CUISINE

bouillabaisse

Cooking time: 50 minutes - Preparation time: 20 minutes

method

1. Remove bones and skin from fish fillets and cut into 2 cm/3/4 in cubes. Peel and devein prawns, leaving tails intact. Scrub and remove beards from mussels. Cut crab into quarters. Set aside.
2. Heat oil in a large saucepan over a medium heat, add garlic, onions and leeks and cook for 5 minutes or until onions are golden. Add tomatoes, thyme, basil, parsley, bay leaves, orange rind, saffron, wine and stock and bring to the boil. Reduce heat and simmer for 30 minutes.
3. Add fish and crab and cook for 10 minutes, add remaining seafood and cook for 5 minutes longer or until fish and seafood are cooked. Season to taste with black pepper.

Serves 6

ingredients

- 3 kg/6 lb mixed fish and seafood, including firm white fish fillets, prawns, mussels, crab and squid rings
- 1/4 cup/60 ml/2 fl oz olive oil
- 2 cloves garlic, crushed
- 2 large onions, chopped
- 2 leeks, sliced
- 2 x 440 g/14 oz canned tomatoes, undrained and mashed
- 1 tablespoon chopped fresh thyme or 1 teaspoon dried thyme
- 2 tablespoons chopped fresh basil or 1 1/2 teaspoons dried basil
- 2 tablespoons chopped fresh parsley
- 2 bay leaves
- 2 tablespoons finely grated orange rind
- 1 teaspoon saffron threads
- 1 cup/250 ml/8 fl oz dry white wine
- 1 cup/250 ml/8 fl oz fish stock
- freshly ground black pepper

tip from the chef

Originally cooked on the beach by fishermen, bouillabaisse is one of the best known and most popular fish soups. It can be made using whatever seafood is available so use this recipe as a guide only. For a complete meal accompany with crusty French bread and a glass of dry white wine.

mussels
in wine and garlic

■□□ | Cooking time: 30 minutes - Preparation time: 5 minutes

ingredients
- 30 g/1 oz butter
- 4 pickling onions or shallots, finely chopped
- 3 cloves garlic, crushed
- 2 cups/500 ml/16 fl oz white wine
- 1 cup/250 ml/8 fl oz fish stock
- 2 kg/4 lb mussels, scrubbed and beards removed
- freshly ground black pepper
- 2 tablespoons finely chopped fresh parsley

method
1. Melt butter in a large saucepan over a medium heat, add onions or shallots and garlic and cook, stirring, for 5 minutes or until onions or shallots are golden. Add wine and stock, bring to the boil, then reduce heat and simmer for 10 minutes.
2. Add mussels and cook for 5 minutes or until shells open. Discard any mussels that do not open after 5 minutes cooking. Using a slotted spoon remove mussels from liquid and place in a serving dish. Season sauce to taste with black pepper, pour over mussels and sprinkle with parsley.

Serves 4

tip from the chef
Mussels will live out of water for up to 7 days if treated correctly. To keep mussels alive, place them in a bucket, cover with a wet towel and top with ice. Store in a cool place and as the ice melts, drain off the water and replace the ice. It is important that the mussels do not sit in the water or they will drown.

soups and starters > 11

12 > FRENCH CUISINE

salad niçoise

soups and starters > 13

Cooking time: 0 minute - Preparation time: 15 minutes

method
1. Arrange lettuce leaves on a large serving platter or in a large salad bowl.
2. Top with beans, red pepper, artichokes, tomatoes, cucumber, spring onions, anchovy fillets, tuna, olives and eggs.
3. Drizzle with oil and season to taste with black pepper.

Serves 4-6

ingredients
- 1 lettuce of your choice, leaves separated
- 500 g/1 lb fresh young broad beans, shelled
- 1 large red pepper, cut into thin strips
- marinated artichoke hearts, halved
- 250 g/8 oz cherry tomatoes
- 1 large cucumber, cut into strips
- 3 spring onions, chopped
- 12 canned anchovy fillets, drained
- 250 g/8 oz canned tuna in water, drained
- 185 g/6 oz marinated black olives
- 6 hard boiled eggs, quartered
- 1/4 cup/60 ml/2 fl oz olive oil
- freshly ground black pepper

tip from the chef
This is an easy Spring or Summer dish. As the broad beans are eaten raw it must be made with very fresh young beans. It should be noted that there are many versions of this salad and that the traditional salad does not include potatoes or other cooked vegetables.

mixed
vegetables with tapenade

■□□ | Cooking time: 0 minute - Preparation time: 15 minutes

ingredients
- 250 g/8 oz small new potatoes, cooked
- 125 g/4 oz green beans, cooked
- 250 g/8 oz asparagus spears, cooked
- 60 g/2 oz snow peas, cooked
- 1 head broccoli, broken into florets, cooked
- 1 lettuce of your choice
- 2 tomatoes, cut into wedges
- 1 red, green or yellow pepper, roasted and cut into pieces
- 2 stalks celery, cut into matchsticks

tapenade
- 125 g/4 oz pitted black olives
- 1 canned anchovy fillet, drained
- 1 tablespoon capers, drained and rinsed
- 2 tablespoons olive oil
- 1 clove garlic, crushed
- 2 teaspoons lemon juice
- 3 tablespoons natural yogurt
- freshly ground black pepper

red wine vinegar dressing
- 1/4 cup/60 ml/2 fl oz red wine vinegar
- 2 tablespoons olive oil
- 1 teaspoon Dijon mustard

method
1. To make tapenade, process olives, anchovy fillet, capers, oil, garlic and lemon juice in a food processor or blender to make a paste. Transfer to a small bowl, add yogurt and black pepper. Cover and refrigerate for 1 hour or until ready to serve.
2. To make dressing, place all ingredients in a screwtop jar and shake well to combine.
3. Arrange all vegetables, attractively, on a large serving platter. Cover and chill. Drizzle with dressing and serve with tapenade.

Serves 8

tip from the chef
Vegetables can be arranged quite elegantly on a white ceramic platter for a formal approach or, for a more rustic one, like casual outdoor entertaining, they can be left fairly chunky and served on a flat wooden or colorful ceramic platter. Olive pâté called tapenade is delicious served on toast or crackers, and it is also a nice alternative to butter as a spread on sandwiches.

soups and starters > 15

16 > FRENCH CUISINE

cheese soufflé

soups and starters > 17

■■□ | Cooking time: 30 minutes - Preparation time: 20 minutes

method

1. Lightly grease four 1 cup/250 ml/8 fl oz capacity soufflé dishes and sprinkle with Parmesan cheese. Set aside.
2. Melt butter in a saucepan over a medium heat, add flour and cook, stirring for 1 minute. Remove pan from heat and gradually whisk in milk. Return pan to heat and cook, stirring constantly, for 5 minutes or until sauce boils and thickens. Remove pan from heat and whisk in egg yolks, one at a time. Stir in Gruyère cheese and black pepper to taste.
3. Place egg whites in a bowl and beat until soft peaks form. Fold egg white mixture into sauce, spoon mixture into prepared soufflé dishes and bake at 200°C/400°F/Gas 6 for 20 minutes or until soufflés are puffed and golden.

ingredients

> 30 g/1 oz Parmesan cheese
> 60 g/2 oz butter
> 1/3 cup/45 g/1 1/2 oz flour
> 1 1/2 cups/375 ml/12 fl oz milk
> 6 egg yolks
> 125 g/4 oz Gruyère cheese
> freshly ground black pepper
> 8 egg whites

Serves 4

tip from the chef

For the best volume have egg whites at room temperature before beating. Egg whites for a soufflé should be beaten until they are stiff, but not dry. The bowl that the egg whites are beaten in must be clean and grease-free or they will not beat up.

chicken
in apple cider

■■□ | Cooking time: 45 minutes - Preparation time: 10 minutes

ingredients

- 1 tablespoon olive oil
- 2 cloves garlic, crushed
- 10 pickling onions or shallots
- 4 boneless chicken breast fillets
- 3 tablespoons fresh tarragon leaves or 1 tablespoon dried tarragon
- 1 cup/250 ml/8 fl oz apple cider
- 1 cup/250 ml/8 fl oz chicken stock
- 1/4 cup/60 ml/2 fl oz dry white wine
- 1 tablespoon tarragon or white wine vinegar
- 1 cup/200 g/6 1/2 oz natural yogurt
- freshly ground black pepper

method

1. Heat oil in a large frying pan over a medium heat, add garlic and onions or shallots and cook, stirring, for 5 minutes. Add chicken and cook, turning, for 10 minutes or until golden on all sides.
2. Add tarragon, cider, stock, wine and vinegar to pan and bring to the boil. Reduce heat, cover and simmer for 30 minutes or until chicken is tender. Remove pan from heat, stir in yogurt and season to taste with black pepper.

Serves 4

tip from the chef

If you do not have apple cider, sparkling or still apple juice can be used instead.

poultry > 19

20 > FRENCH CUISINE

poultry

duck
à l'orange

Cooking time: 1 hour 10 minutes - Preparation time: 20 minutes

method

1. Season duck with black pepper and place rosemary, thyme and garlic in cavity. Pierce skin of duck several times with a fork and brush with oil. Place duck on a wire rack set in a heatproof baking dish and bake at 180°C/350°F/Gas 4 for 1 hour or until tender. Remove duck from pan, cover, set aside and keep warm.
2. Skim fat from pan juices, stir in orange juice, orange rind, sugar, orange segments and brandy and bring to the boil. Reduce heat and simmer, stirring, for 10 minutes or until sauce is reduced by one-third.
3. To serve, carve duck, arrange on a serving platter and pour over sauce.

ingredients

- 2 kg/4 lb duck
- freshly ground black pepper
- 2 sprigs fresh rosemary or 1/2 teaspoon dried rosemary
- 2 sprigs fresh thyme or 1/2 teaspoon dried thyme
- 1 clove garlic, crushed
- 1 tablespoon olive oil
- 2 cups/500 ml/16 fl oz orange juice
- 1 tablespoon finely grated orange rind
- 1 tablespoon brown sugar
- 3 oranges, segmented and all white pith removed
- 2 tablespoons brandy

Serves 6

tip from the chef

This recipe is a modern version of an old favorite. The richness of the duck is balanced by the tartness of the orange. Serve it with a steamed green vegetable and small new potatoes.

blackcurrant pheasant

Cooking time: 50 minutes - Preparation time: 15 minutes

ingredients

- 1.5 kg/3 lb pheasant, quartered
- freshly ground black pepper
- 1/2 cup/125 ml/4 fl oz water
- 1 tablespoon olive oil
- 2 tablespoons blackcurrant conserve
- 1/2 cup/125 ml/4 fl oz orange juice
- 1 cup/250 ml/8 fl oz chicken stock
- 1/2 cup/125 ml/4 fl oz red wine

glazed vegetables

- 12 small carrots, scrubbed
- 12 small turnips, scrubbed
- 12 pickling onions or shallots
- 12 small new potatoes, scrubbed
- 1 tablespoon honey
- 2 tablespoons olive oil

method

1. Season pheasant with black pepper and place on a rack set in a heatproof baking dish. Pour water into dish.
2. Place oil, conserve and orange juice in a small bowl and mix to combine. Brush pheasant with conserve mixture and bake at 180°C/350°F/Gas 4, basting frequently, for 40 minutes or until pheasant is tender.
3. To make glazed vegetables, place carrots, turnips, onions and potatoes in a lightly greased baking dish. Place honey and oil in a small bowl and mix to combine. Brush vegetables with honey mixture and bake at 200°C/400°F/Gas 6, basting frequently, for 30 minutes or until vegetables are cooked.
4. Remove pheasant from pan, cover, set aside and keep warm. Skim fat from pan juices, add stock and wine and any remaining conserve mixture to pan, place over a medium heat and bring to the boil, stirring constantly for 3-4 minutes or until sauce reduces and thickens slightly. Pour sauce over pheasant and serve immediately, with vegetables.

Serves 4

tip from the chef

This is a simple yet tasty method of preparing pheasant. Other vegetables you might like to glaze are small zucchini, eggplant and parsnips. Zucchini will only take about 15 minutes to cook.

poultry > 23

24 > FRENCH CUISINE

coq au vin

a

poultry > 25

■■□ | Cooking time: 2 hours - Preparation time: 10 minutes

method

1. Toss chicken in flour to coat (a). Shake off excess flour and set aside.
2. Heat oil in a large nonstick frying pan over a medium heat and cook chicken in batches (b), turning frequently, for 10 minutes or until brown on all sides. Remove chicken from pan and drain on absorbent kitchen paper.
3. Add garlic, onions or shallots and bacon to pan and cook, stirring, for 5 minutes or until onions are golden. Return chicken to pan, stir in stock and wine (c) and bring to the boil. Reduce heat, cover and simmer, stirring occasionally, for 1 1/4 hour or until chicken is tender. Add mushrooms and black pepper to taste and cook for 10 minutes longer (d).

Serves 6

ingredients

> 2 kg/4 lb chicken pieces
> 1/2 cup/60 g/2 oz seasoned flour
> 2 tablespoons olive oil
> 2 cloves garlic, crushed
> 12 pickling onions or shallots, peeled
> 8 rashers bacon, chopped
> 1 cup/250 ml/8 fl oz chicken stock
> 3 cups/750 ml/1 1/4 pt red wine
> 250 g/8 oz button mushrooms
> freshly ground black pepper

tip from the chef

Serve coq au vin with braised artichokes and beans (page 50) and steamed new potatoes.

b

c

d

lamb with roasted garlic sauce

■■■ | Cooking time: 2 hours 10 minutes - Preparation time: 30 minutes

ingredients

- 1 head of garlic, cloves separated and peeled
- 4 canned anchovy fillets, drained
- olive oil
- freshly ground black pepper
- 2 kg/4 lb leg of lamb, trimmed of excess fat
- 1 onion, finely chopped
- 1 carrot, finely chopped
- 2 stalks celery, finely chopped
- 1/2 cup/125 ml/4 fl oz dry white wine
- 1 cup/250 ml/8 fl oz chicken stock
- 2 tablespoons chopped fresh parsley

tip from the chef

While this recipe uses a lot of garlic, you will find that roasted garlic has a subtle and sweet flavor.

method

1. Place 4 cloves garlic, anchovy fillets, 1 teaspoon oil and black pepper to taste in a food processor or blender and process to make a smooth paste.
2. Using a sharp knife make several slits in the lamb. Push a little paste into each slit, then rub remaining paste over surface of lamb. Set aside to marinate for 20-30 minutes or in the refrigerator overnight.
3. Place onion, carrot, celery, wine and remaining garlic in a frying pan and cook, stirring, for 5 minutes.
4. Place lamb in a baking dish. Pour wine mixture into dish and bake at 180°C/350°F/Gas 4, adding more wine to keep vegetables moist if necessary, for 1 1/2-2 hours or until lamb is cooked to your liking. Transfer lamb to a large serving platter and set aside to keep warm.
5. Skim fat from cooking juices remaining in baking dish. Place juices with vegetables and garlic in a food processor or blender and process until smooth. Transfer mixture to a small saucepan, stir in stock and bring to the boil over a medium heat, reduce heat and simmer for 5 minutes or until sauce reduces and thickens and coats the back of a spoon. Stir in parsley and season to taste with black pepper. To serve, carve lamb and accompany with sauce.

Serves 6

meat > 27

28 > FRENCH CUISINE

roast
pork with fennel

meat

■■■ | Cooking time: 1 hour 10 minutes - Preparation time: 20 minutes

method

1. Unroll loin and make a cut in the middle of the fleshy part of the meat and lay out. Score rind at 2 cm/3/4 in intervals. Place pork, rind side down, and top with a layer of fennel slices, leaving a 2 cm/3/4 in border. Sprinkle with half the fennel seeds and sage. Season with black pepper. Roll loin and tie with string. Place in a glass or ceramic dish, pour over wine, cover and marinate in the refrigerator overnight.
2. Remove pork from wine mixture and place on a wire rack set in a flameproof baking dish. Reserve wine mixture. Sprinkle pork with remaining fennel seeds and sage and bake at 180°C/350°F/Gas 4 for 1 hour or until tender. Remove and set aside.
3. Pour reserved wine mixture into baking dish and bring to the boil over a high heat, stirring and scraping base of dish, for 2-3 minutes or until mixture reduces slightly. Slice pork, spoon over sauce and sprinkle with fennel leaves.

ingredients

> 1.5 kg/3 lb boneless pork loin
> 1 fennel bulb, thinly sliced
> 1 teaspoon fennel seeds
> 2 teaspoons fresh sage or 1 teaspoon dried sage
> freshly ground black pepper
> 1 cup/250 ml/8 fl oz dry white wine
> 2 tablespoons chopped fresh fennel leaves

Serves 8

tip from the chef

When scoring pork rind take care not to cut too deeply. The cut should only be about 5 mm/1/4 in deep. Scoring makes the rind easier to cut when it is cooked.

navarin lamb

Cooking time: 2 hours 50 minutes - Preparation time: 20 minutes

ingredients
- 6 lamb noisettes or loin chops
- 1 onion, sliced
- 1 clove garlic, crushed
- 1 teaspoon chopped fresh rosemary or 1/2 teaspoon dried rosemary
- 440 g/14 oz canned tomatoes, undrained and mashed
- 1 cup/250 ml/8 fl oz chicken stock
- 1/2 cup/125 ml/4 fl oz dry red wine
- 12 small new potatoes
- 12 pickling onions or shallots
- 6 small carrots, scrubbed
- 250 g/8 oz green beans, cut into 5 cm/2 in pieces
- freshly ground black pepper

method
1. Heat a nonstick frying pan over a medium heat, add lamb and cook for 3-4 minutes each side or until brown. Remove lamb from pan and place in a casserole dish.
2. Add sliced onion, garlic, rosemary and 1 tablespoon juice from tomatoes to pan and cook over a medium heat, stirring, for 5 minutes or until onion is soft. Stir tomatoes, stock and wine into pan, bring to the boil, then reduce heat and simmer for 15 minutes or until mixture reduces and thickens. Add sauce to casserole, cover and bake at 180°C/350°F/Gas 4 for 1 hour. Add potatoes and pickling onions or shallots to casserole and bake for 1 hour longer or until meat and vegetables are tender.
3. Boil or microwave carrots and beans until just tender, drain and refresh under cold running water. Add carrots and beans to casserole and bake for 20 minutes longer. Season to taste with black pepper.

Serves 6

tip from the chef
Lamb noisettes are rolled, boneless loin chops. The meat is rolled up tightly and tied. These are readily available in the meat section of your supermarket and you will find that most butchers are happy to prepare noisettes for you if you order them in advance.

meat > 31

32 > FRENCH CUISINE

fruit-filled pork

meat

■■■ | Cooking time: 1 hour 50 minutes - Preparation time: 20 minutes

method

1. Using a sharp knife, separate bones from meat, leaving both ends intact, to make a pocket. Trim excess fat from outside of rack.
2. Place blueberries or blackcurrants in a bowl and season to taste with black pepper. Place half the fruit mixture in pocket of meat and place in a flameproof baking dish. Brush pork with oil and bake at 220°C/425°F/Gas 7 for 20 minutes. Reduce oven temperature to 200°C/400°F/Gas 6 and bake for 1 hour longer or until cooked. Remove meat from pan, place on a warm serving platter, cover with foil and set aside to stand for 15-20 minutes.
3. Add wine and remaining fruit to baking dish and bring to the boil over a medium heat. Reduce heat and simmer, stirring constantly and scraping base of dish, for 10 minutes or until sauce is reduced by half. Serve sauce with pork.

ingredients

- > 1 rack of pork, containing 8 cutlets
- > 500 g/1 lb blueberries or blackcurrants
- > freshly ground black pepper
- > 1 tablespoon olive oil
- > 1 cup/250 ml/8 fl oz dry white wine

Serves 8

tip from the chef

A tasty and easy dish that can use a variety of fruit. Try cherries, redcurrants or plums instead of the blueberries or blackcurrants.

blanquette of veal

Cooking time: 1 hour 45 minutes - **Preparation time:** 25 minutes

ingredients

- 1 kg/2 lb diced veal
- 1 bouquet garni
- 1 onion, finely chopped
- 1 carrot, finely chopped
- 2 stalks celery, finely chopped
- 4 cups/1 liter/1 3/4 pt cold chicken stock
- 6 pickling onions or shallots
- 6 small carrots, scrubbed
- 12 small new potatoes
- 1 tablespoon olive oil
- 250 g/8 oz button mushrooms
- 1/2 cup/125 ml/4 fl oz dry white wine
- 2 teaspoons cornflour blended with
- 1/4 cup/60 ml/2 fl oz cream
- 125 g/4 oz frozen petit pois (small peas)
- 2 tablespoons lemon juice
- 2 tablespoons natural yogurt
- 3 tablespoons chopped fresh parsley
- freshly ground black pepper

method

1. Bring a saucepan of water to the boil. Add meat and boil for 2 minutes. Drain meat, rinse under cold running water and drain again. Place meat, bouquet garni, onion, carrot, celery and stock in a clean saucepan. Bring to the boil, then simmer for 45 minutes. Add pickling onions or shallots, carrots and potatoes and cook until tender.
2. Heat oil in a frying pan, add mushrooms and stir 5 minutes. Add wine, cover and simmer 5 minutes. Remove lid and simmer until juices are reduced by half. Set aside.
3. Using a slotted spoon remove meat and whole vegetables from stock mixture. Strain stock and discard bouquet garni and chopped vegetables. Return stock to a clean pan and boil for 15 minutes or until reduced to 1 cup/250 ml/8 fl oz. Stir in cornflour mixture and cook, stirring, until sauce thickens slightly.
4. Add mushroom mixture, meat, vegetables and peas and cook, stirring occasionally, for 5 minutes or until peas are cooked. Stir in lemon juice, yogurt, parsley and black pepper to taste and bring back to simmering before serving.

Serves 6

tip from the chef

A traditional blanquette is enriched with egg yolks and cream. In this version the egg yolks are replaced with yogurt and the cream is greatly reduced to give a dish that is just as tasty as the original, but much lighter in fat and calories.

pot-au-feu

meat

Cooking time: 3 hours 35 minutes - Preparation time: 20 minutes

method
1. Place beef, clove-studded onion, black peppercorns, garlic and bouquet garni in a large saucepan. Add cold water to cover and bring to the boil over a medium heat, remove any scum as necessary. Reduce heat, cover and simmer for 2½-3 hours.
2. Add potatoes, carrots, parsnips, celery and leeks to pan and simmer for 20-30 minutes or until vegetables are tender.
3. Remove meat and vegetables from cooking liquid, set aside and keep warm.
4. Strain cooking liquid and discard clove-studded onion, black peppercorns, garlic and bouquet garni. Return cooking liquid to saucepan, add wine, bring to the boil and simmer for 5 minutes. To serve, slice meat and arrange with vegetables on a large serving platter. Place cooking liquid in a soup tureen and pass separately.

ingredients
- 2-2.5 kg/4-5 lb topside of beef
- 1 onion, studded with
- 4 cloves
- ½ teaspoon black peppercorns
- 2 cloves garlic
- 1 bouquet garni
- 4 large potatoes, quartered
- 4 large carrots, cut into 5 cm/2 in pieces
- 4 parsnips, cut into 5 cm/2 in pieces
- 8 stalks celery, cut into 5 cm/2 in pieces
- 4 thin leeks, cut into 5 cm/2 in pieces
- ½ cup/125 ml/4 fl oz red wine

Serves 8

tip from the chef
This is a wonderfully economical dish to make for a crowd. Serve the meat, vegetables and broth together in soup plates. Accompany with French bread and a selection of mustards and pickles. You can prepare this dish to the end of step 1 the day before, then about 1 hour before serving, remove the layer of fat that has set on the surface, bring to the boil and complete as described in recipe.

beef bourguignon

| Cooking time: 2 hours 20 minutes - Preparation time: 15 minutes

ingredients

- 1 kg/2 lb chuck steak, trimmed of all visible fat and cut into 2.5 cm/1 in cubes
- 2 cups/500 ml/16 fl oz dry red wine
- 1 teaspoon chopped fresh thyme
- 2 cloves garlic, crushed
- 1 bay leaf
- 1 tablespoon olive oil
- 2 rashers bacon, trimmed of all visible fat and chopped
- 250 g/8 oz button mushrooms
- 12 pickling onions or shallots
- 1 cup/250 ml/8 fl oz beef stock
- 1/2 cup/125 ml/4 fl oz tomato purée
- 2 tablespoons brandy
- 2 teaspoons cornflour blended with 2 tablespoons water
- freshly ground black pepper

method

1. Combine beef, wine, thyme, garlic and bay leaf in a glass or ceramic bowl (a), cover and marinate for 30 minutes. Remove beef from wine mixture and pat dry. Reserve wine mixture.
2. Heat oil in a large saucepan over a high heat, add beef and bacon in batches (b) and cook for 5 minutes or until brown. Remove beef mixture from pan, drain on absorbent kitchen paper and set aside.
3. Add mushrooms and onions or shallots to pan (c) and cook, stirring, for 5 minutes or until onions or shallots are brown. Remove mushrooms and onions from pan and set aside.
4. Return beef mixture to pan, stir in stock, tomato purée and reserved wine mixture, bring to simmering, cover and simmer for 1 1/2 hours or until beef is tender. Return mushrooms and onions or shallots to pan (d), stir in brandy and cornflour mixture, cover and simmer for 30 minutes longer. Season to taste with black pepper.

Serves 6

tip from the chef

This classic French stew is even better if you have time to marinate it in the red wine and herbs overnight.

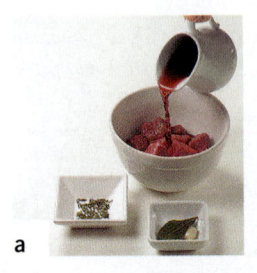

a

meat > 39

b c d

40 > FRENCH CUISINE

rabbit with thyme and mustard

■ ■ □ | Cooking time: 2 hours 10 minutes - Preparation time: 10 minutes

method

1. Heat oil in a large saucepan over a medium heat, add rabbit and cook, turning frequently, for 10 minutes or until brown on all sides.
2. Add mustard, stock, wine and thyme to pan and bring to the boil. Reduce heat, cover and simmer, stirring occasionally, for 1½ hours or until rabbit is tender. Add potatoes and cook for 30 minutes longer or until potatoes are tender. Season to taste with black pepper.

Serves 4

ingredients

- 2 tablespoons olive oil
- 1 kg/2 lb rabbit, cut into pieces
- 3 tablespoons Dijon mustard
- 3 cups/750 ml/1¼ pt chicken stock
- ½ cup/125 ml/4 fl oz red wine
- 6 sprigs fresh thyme or 1 teaspoon dried thyme
- 250 g/8 oz small new potatoes
- freshly ground black pepper

tip from the chef

Rabbit and mustard are traditional companions –this recipe is a variation of a popular 17th-century French dish, rabbit stew in mustard sauce.

steak bordelaise

Cooking time: 20 minutes - Preparation time: 15 minutes

ingredients
- 6 fillet or rib-eye steaks
- 6 spring onions, chopped
- 1 clove garlic, crushed
- 1 cup/250 ml/8 fl oz beef stock
- 1/2 cup/125 ml/4 fl oz dry red wine
- freshly ground black pepper

method
1. Heat a nonstick frying pan over a medium heat, add steaks and cook for 3-4 minutes each side or until cooked to your liking. Remove steaks from pan, set aside and keep warm.
2. Add spring onions, garlic and 2 tablespoons stock to pan and cook, stirring, for 2-3 minutes. Remove spring onions from pan and set aside. Add remaining stock and wine to pan, bring to the boil and boil for 5-10 minutes or until sauce reduces and thickens. Return spring onions to pan and season to taste with black pepper. Serve sauce with steak.

Serves 6

tip from the chef
This dish takes little time or effort to prepare and is excellent for mid-week entertaining. It is delicious served with potato gratin and glazed vegetables (page 22).

meat > 43

44 > FRENCH CUISINE

sausages with onions and wine

meat

> 45

■☐☐ | Cooking time: 35 minutes - Preparation time: 10 minutes

method

1. Heat a nonstick frying pan over a medium heat, add sausages and cook, turning until brown on all sides and almost cooked. Remove from pan and drain on absorbent kitchen paper.
2. Add onions, garlic and 2 tablespoons wine to pan and cook, stirring and adding wine as necessary for 15-20 minutes or until onions are very soft and golden.
3. Return sausages to pan, stir in remaining wine and cook for 5-10 minutes longer or until sausages are cooked. Season with black pepper.

ingredients

- > 8 thin sausages of your choice
- > 2 large onions, thinly sliced
- > 1 clove garlic, crushed
- > 1 cup/250 ml/8 fl oz dry white wine
- > freshly ground black pepper

Serves 4

tip from the chef

You can make this dish using any type of sausage. If chicken or turkey sausages are available, use these as they are lower in fat than traditional meat-based sausages. For a complete meal serve with fennel and pea purée and mashed potatoes or crusty bread.

beans
in rich tomato sauce

Cooking time: 1 hour 50 minutes - Preparation time: 10 minutes

ingredients
- 500 g/1 lb dried lima beans
- 1 tablespoon olive oil
- 1 clove garlic, crushed
- 1 onion, finely chopped
- 3 tablespoons chopped fresh parsley
- 1 tablespoon chopped fresh rosemary or 1 teaspoon dried rosemary
- 440 g/14 oz canned tomatoes, undrained and mashed
- freshly ground black pepper

method
1. Place beans in a large bowl, cover with water and set aside to soak overnight.
2. Drain beans, place in a saucepan with enough water to cover and bring to the boil. Boil for 10 minutes, then reduce heat and simmer for 1 hour or until tender. Drain and set aside.
3. Heat oil in a large saucepan, add garlic and onion and cook, stirring, for 3 minutes or until onion is golden. Add parsley, rosemary and tomatoes and bring to the boil. Reduce heat and simmer, stirring occasionally, for 20 minutes or until mixture reduces and thickens. Stir in beans and black pepper to taste and cook for 15 minutes longer.

Serves 6

tip from the chef
This dish also makes a good vegetarian main meal. If so, it will serve 4; accompany with crusty bread and a tossed green salad.

vegetables > 47

48 > FRENCH CUISINE

ratatouille

vegetables

■☐☐ | Cooking time: 30 minutes - Preparation time: 15 minutes

method
1. Place eggplant slices in a colander set over a bowl and sprinkle with salt. Set aside to stand for 10 minutes, then rinse under cold running water and pat dry with absorbent kitchen paper.
2. Heat oil in a nonstick frying pan over a medium heat. Add garlic and onion and cook, stirring, for 3 minutes or until onion is golden.
3. Add eggplant slices to pan and cook, a few at a time, for 5 minutes each side or until brown. Return eggplant to pan, add red pepper, green pepper, zucchini, tomatoes and olives and bring to the boil. Reduce heat and simmer for 20 minutes or until mixture reduces and thickens. Season to taste with black pepper.

ingredients
- 2 eggplant, cut into 1 cm/$1/2$ in thick slices
- salt
- 1 tablespoon olive oil
- 2 cloves garlic, crushed
- 1 large onion, cut into wedges
- 1 large red pepper, chopped
- 1 large green pepper, chopped
- 3 zucchini, sliced
- 440 g/14 oz canned tomatoes, undrained and mashed
- 90 g/3 oz black olives
- freshly ground black pepper

Serves 4

tip from the chef
Ratatouille is a versatile dish that can be served as an accompaniment to a meal, as a first course or as a light meal with crusty bread. Serve it hot, warm or cold. If you make it in advance and reheat it, it tastes even better.

50 > FRENCH CUISINE

braised
artichokes and beans

vegetables

■□□ | Cooking time: 15 minutes - Preparation time: 10 minutes

method
1. Melt butter in a frying pan over a medium heat, add garlic and onions and cook, stirring, for 3 minutes or until onions are soft.
2. Add carrots, beans, artichokes and stock and bring to the boil. Reduce heat and simmer for 10 minutes or until vegetables are tender. Season to taste with black pepper.

Serves 6

ingredients
- 30 g/l 1 oz butter
- 2 cloves garlic, crushed
- 2 onions, sliced
- 2 carrots, sliced
- 250 g/8 oz fresh broad beans, shelled, or 125 g/4 oz frozen broad beans
- 440 g/ 14 oz canned artichoke hearts, drained
- 1 cup/250 ml/8 fl oz vegetable stock
- freshly ground black pepper

tip from the chef
Broad beans, also known as fava beans, are one of the oldest cultivated vegetables in the Western world and have played a major role in the cuisine of the Mediterranean for centuries.

crêpes suzette

Cooking time: 25 minutes - Preparation time: 25 minutes

ingredients
- 1/2 cup/125 ml/4 fl oz orange juice, warmed
- 2 tablespoons caster sugar
- 1 tablespoon orange-flavored liqueur
- 1 tablespoon brandy

crêpes
- 1 cup/125 g/4 oz flour
- 3/4 cup/185 ml/6 fl oz milk
- 1/2 cup/125 ml/4 fl oz water
- 2 eggs
- 15 g/1/2 oz butter, melted
- 1 tablespoon sugar

method
1. To make crêpes, place flour, milk, water, eggs, butter and sugar in a food processor or blender and process until smooth. Cover and set aside to stand for 1 hour.
2. Pour 2-3 tablespoons batter into a heated, lightly greased 18 cm/7 in crêpe pan and tilt pan so batter covers base thinly and evenly. Cook over a high heat for 1 minute or until lightly browned. Turn crêpe and cook on second side for 30 seconds. Remove from pan, set aside and keep warm. Repeat with remaining batter to make 12 crêpes.
3. Fold crêpes into quarters and arrange overlapping in a heatproof dish. Pour over orange juice and sprinkle with caster sugar. Place orange liqueur and brandy in a small saucepan and warm over a low heat, ignite, pour over crêpes and serve immediately.

Serves 4

tip from the chef
To keep cooked crêpes warm while making the rest of the batch, place the crêpes in a stack on a heatproof plate and place in a low oven, or over a saucepan of simmering water. Alcohol needs to be warmed to flambé effectively; however, take care not to overheat or it will evaporate before you can ignite it.

desserts > 53

plum clafoutis

desserts

■□□ | Cooking time: 45 minutes - Preparation time: 10 minutes

method
1. Arrange plums, cut side down, in a lightly greased 25 cm/10 in flan dish.
2. Sift flour into a bowl and make a well in the center. Break eggs into well, add caster sugar and milk and mix to form a smooth batter.
3. Pour batter over plums and bake at 180°C/350°F/Gas 4 for 45 minutes or until firm and golden. Serve hot, warm or cold, sprinkled with icing sugar.

ingredients
> 500 g/1 lb dark plums, halved and stoned, or 440 g/14 oz canned plums, well drained
> 1 cup/125 g/4 oz self-raising flour
> 3 eggs
> 1/2 cup/100 g/3 1/2 oz caster sugar
> 1/2 cup/125 ml/4 fl oz milk
> 1 tablespoon icing sugar, sifted

Serves 6

tip from the chef
Clafoutis can be made with any fruit that you wish. Apricots and cherries are also popular choices.

raspberry mousse

Cooking time: 0 minute - **Preparation time:** 20 minutes

ingredients

- 500 g/1 lb fresh or frozen raspberries
- 2 teaspoons gelatin dissolved in 2 tablespoons hot water, cooled
- 125 g/4 oz ricotta cheese, drained
- 4 eggs, separated
- 1/4 cup/60 g/2 oz caster sugar
- chocolate curls, to garnish (optional)

method

1. Place raspberries in a food processor or blender and process to make a purée. Push purée through a sieve to remove seeds and set aside. Stir gelatin mixture into purée (a) and set aside.
2. Place ricotta or curd cheese in a food processor or blender and process until smooth. Set aside.
3. Place egg yolks and sugar in a heatproof bowl, set over a saucepan of simmering water and beat (b) until a ribbon trail forms when beater is lifted from mixture. Remove bowl from heat. Whisk egg yolk mixture, then ricotta cheese into raspberry purée (c). Cover and chill until just beginning to set.
4. Place egg whites in a bowl and beat until stiff peaks form. Fold egg white mixture into fruit mixture (d). Spoon mousse mixture into 4 lightly oiled 1/2 cup/125 ml/4 fl oz capacity molds or ramekins, cover and chill until set. To serve, garnish with chocolate curls.

Serves 4

tip from the chef

To make chocolate curls, using a vegetable peeler, shave the sides of a block of chocolate. For curls to form, the chocolate should be at room temperature. If the chocolate is chilled, shavings will form.

a

desserts > 57

58 > FRENCH CUISINE

chocolate
soufflé

■■□ | Cooking time 30 minutes - Preparation time: 15 minutes

method

1. Sift cornflour and almonds together into a bowl and make a well in the center.
2. Place milk and coffee in saucepan and bring to the boil over a medium heat. Slowly whisk milk mixture into almond mixture (a) and continue whisking until smooth. Return to saucepan and stir over a medium heat. As soon as mixture comes to the boil, remove from heat.
3. Stir chocolate and caster sugar into milk mixture (b) and continue stirring until chocolate melts. Whisk egg yolks (c) and liqueur into milk mixture, cover and set aside to keep warm.
4. Place egg whites in a bowl and beat until soft peaks form. Gradually beat in brown sugar and continue beating until stiff peaks form. Whisk one-third of the egg white mixture into the chocolate mixture (d), then fold in remaining egg white mixture.
5. Pour soufflé mixture into a greased 20 cm/8 in soufflé dish and bake at 180°C/350°F/Gas 4 for 20 minutes or until well risen. Sprinkle with icing sugar and serve immediately.

Serves 6

ingredients

- 1/4 cup/30 g/1 oz cornflour
- 30 g/1 oz ground almonds
- 1/4 cup/185 ml/6 fl oz milk
- 1 tablespoon strong black coffee
- 75 g/2 1/2 oz dark chocolate, broken into pieces
- 2 teaspoons caster sugar
- 2 egg yolks
- 1 tablespoon coffee-flavored liqueur
- 4 egg whites
- 1 tablespoon brown sugar
- 1 tablespoon icing sugar, sifted

tip from the chef

Egg whites at room temperature beat up more rapidly and have a better volume than those straight out of the refrigerator. Correctly beaten egg whites will increase by 7-8 times their original volume.

french
apple tart

Cooking time: 1 hour 30 minutes - Preparation time: 45 minutes

ingredients
- shortcrust pastry
- 2 green apples, peeled and cored
- 1 tablespoon lemon juice
- 1 tablespoon caster sugar

apple filling
- 750 g/1½ lb green apples, peeled, cored and chopped
- 1 cup/250 ml/8 fl oz water
- 2 tablespoons caster sugar
- 30 g/1 oz butter
- ½ teaspoon ground cinnamon
- ½ teaspoon ground nutmeg
- 1 tablespoon lemon juice
- 1 teaspoon finely grated lemon rind
- 1 tablespoon brandy

apricot glaze
- 3 tablespoons apricot jam, sieved

tip from the chef
The easiest way to cut apples into neat slices is to first cut the apple into quarters, then to slice it.

method
1. To make filling, place chopped apples and water in a heavy-based saucepan, cover and cook over a medium heat, stirring frequently, until apples are very soft. Turn into a sieve set over a bowl and drain for 10 minutes. Reserve juices.
2. Place cooked apples, caster sugar, butter, cinnamon, nutmeg, lemon juice, lemon rind and brandy in a food processor or blender and process to make a purée. Cook purée over a low heat, stirring frequently, until a thick paste forms. Set aside to cool completely.
3. Roll out pastry to 5 mm/¼ in thick and large enough to line a 23 cm/9 in flan tin. Rest pastry for 10 minutes, then line tin and chill for 10 minutes. Line pastry case with nonstick baking paper, fill with uncooked rice and bake at 190°C/375°F/Gas 5 for 15 minutes. Remove rice and paper and bake for 5 minutes longer. Set aside to cool.
4. Cut remaining apples into neat slices and toss in lemon juice. Spread purée over base of pastry case. Arrange apple slices overlapping on top of purée, sprinkle with caster sugar and bake for 25-30 minutes or until apples are tender.
5. To make glaze, cook apricot jam and 1 tablespoon reserved apple juice in a small saucepan over a low heat, stirring, for 5 minutes or until a thick syrupy glaze forms. Brush hot glaze over hot tart and set aside to cool. Serve warm or cold.

Serves 8

bakery > 61

62 > FRENCH CUISINE

french
madeleines

Cooking time: 15 minutes - Preparation time: 10 minutes

method
1. Place eggs and sugar in a heatproof bowl set over a saucepan of simmering water and beat until a ribbon trail forms when beater is lifted from mixture. Remove bowl from heat, beat in orange flower water (if using) and continue beating for 2 minutes longer.
2. Sift flour over egg mixture and fold in. Fold butter into batter and divide mixture between 12 greased and floured madeleine tins.
3. Bake at 200°C/400°F/Gas 6 for 10-12 minutes or until madeleines are cooked and golden. Stand in tins for 1 minute before turning onto a wire rack to cool.

ingredients
> 2 eggs
> 1/4 cup/60 g/2 oz caster sugar
> 1 teaspoon orange flower water (optional)
> 1/2 cup/60 g/2 oz flour, sifted
> 60 g/2 oz butter, melted and cooled

Makes 12

tip from the chef

Madeleine tins are available from specialty cookware shops. They come in a sheet (like patty cake tins) and have elongated shell-shaped depressions.

Madeleines are delicious served with desserts such as raspberry mousse (page 56) or as an afternoon treat. They will keep in an airtight container for up to a week and also freeze well.

index

Introduction 3

Soup and starters
Bouillabaisse 8
Cheese soufflé 16
French onion soup 6
Mixed vegetables with tapenade 14
Mussels in wine and garlic 10
Salad Niçoise 12

Poultry
Blackcurrant pheasant 22
Chicken in apple cider 18
Coq au vin 24
Duck à l'orange 20

Meat
Beef Bourguignon 38
Blanquette of veal 34
Fruit-filled pork 32
Lamb with roasted garlic sauce 26
Navarin lamb 30
Pot-au-feu 36
Rabbit with thyme and mustard 40
Roast pork with fennel 28
Sausages with onions and wine 44
Steak Bordelaise 42

Vegetables
Beans in rich tomato sauce 46
Braised artichokes and beans 50
Ratatouille 48

Desserts
Chocolate soufflé 58
Crêpes Suzette 52
Plum clafoutis 54
Raspberry mousse 56

Bakery
French apple tart 60
French madeleines 62